Soul of Vienna

A GUIDE TO EXCEPTIONAL EXPERIENCES

WOLFGANG REITTER AND BARBARA KADLETZ
PHOTOS BY GEORG MOEHRKE

JONGLEZ PUBLISHING
Travel guides

‘AS WE HAVE JUST SEEN,
VIENNA IS AN EXCELLENT PLACE
TO EXPLORE THE ENTIRE COSMOS
IN INNER SOLITUDE.’

PETER CAMPA

Living in Vienna is a special thing, because Vienna is a city full of contrasting diversity. It has so much to offer anyone who goes through life with open eyes and an open mind. In Vienna you can find such an uncomplicated zest for life, a great deal of everyday pleasure, but also intellectual depth and aesthetic fulfilment. Vienna is simply a city that knows how to inspire self-absorbed hedonists just as much as culture-oriented intellectuals.

We don't want to direct our readers to places where they'll encounter every typical Viennese cliché. Instead, we want to offer them places where this fabulous city combines its inherent charm and historic beauty with the creativity of its inhabitants in a very special way – places where this diverse Viennese culture is magnificent, endearing and touching in its own unique way, and where we ourselves love to spend time.

Don't hesitate to follow us to the outermost edges of the city (and beyond). You'll discover wonderful things there. Did you know that parts of Vienna are located in one of the most beautiful nature reserves in Central Europe? That seemingly old-fashioned craftsmanship of the highest quality is a concept for the future, especially in the 21st century? Or how about the 20th-century urbanism that has imprinted its timeless beauty on all places in a subtle manner?

But don't worry, we'll also take you to the historic centre and the many smaller urban hotspots. There you can experience Viennese city life in all its unadulterated uniqueness and vitality. Dive in, wander off, pause – it won't be long before you too are enchanted by this wonderful city!

Wolfgang Reitter and Barbara Kadletz

WHAT YOU WON'T FIND IN THIS GUIDE

- Places where you can admire dead Habsburgs ...
- ... and certainly no memories of Empress Sisi
- Instructions on how to waltz
- Recipes for making a delicious Viennese schnitzel
- Directions to well-known palaces and churches

WHAT YOU WILL FIND IN THIS GUIDE

- traditional Viennese cafés without the tourist crowds
- where to spend the night in a luxury dormitory
- where to sing with an Austrian football legend
- a charming hotel where every room is unique
- a music shop where you can record your own vinyl
- the best ice cream in Vienna
- one of the best-stocked vintage fashion shops in the world
- a magnificent Renaissance palace that even many locals don't know about
- a church that may have inspired Minecraft
- where to enjoy an exceptional goulash

SYMBOLS OF **VIENNA**

Budget friendly

Mid-range

Expensive

Accesible by public transport

Reservations recommended

100% Vienna

Opening times often vary,
so we recommend checking them directly
on the website of the place you plan to visit.

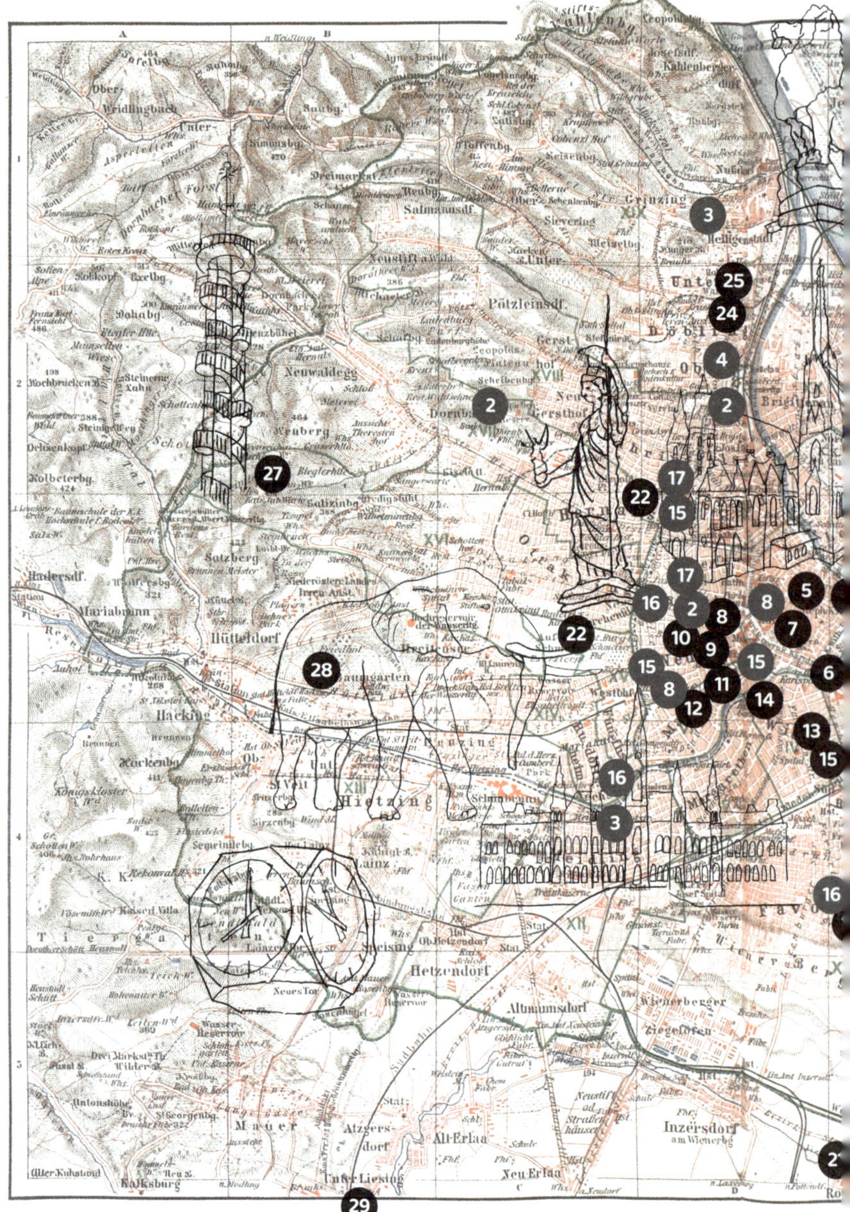

Hütteldorf
Hacking
Hietzing
Hetzendorf
Altmannsdorf
Atzgersdorf
Mauer
Kalksburg
Inzersdorf am Wienerbg
Grinzing
Sievering
Neuwaldegg
Pötzleinsdf.
Heiligenstadt
Salmannsdf.
Wienerberger Ziegelöfen
Unter Liesing
Alt-Erlaa
Neu-Erlaa
Neues Tor

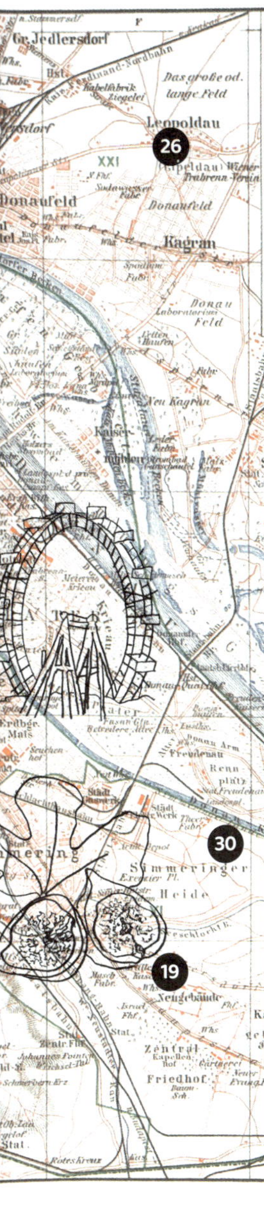

30 EXPERIENCES

01. Bike rental in style
02. A daily pot of goulash
03. A swimming pool on the river
04. A very sophisticated lunch
05. The night bar not to miss!
06. A night in a luxury dormitory
07. Traditional crafts, sugary sweet
08. A boutique hotel where every room is unique
09. Espresso, sauerkraut, and the best croissants in town
10. A chamber of wonders of photography
11. Pure joy
12. A refuge for body and soul
13. One of the best vintage fashion shops in the world
14. An amazing musical treasure trove
15. A traditional Viennese café without the tourist crowds
16. High horse on a flat plate
17. Gelati! Gelati!
18. Ordinary people's amusement park
19. A hidden Renaissance gem
20. Vienna's 'Central Park' on the southern outskirts
21. Slow food at the snail farm
22. One of Vienna's most beautiful beer gardens
23. Let it snow!
24. Big in Japan
25. The oldest restaurant in the city
26. Luxury footwear in a 16th-century castle
27. The heart of Central Europe at your feet
28. A church that may have inspired Minecraft
29. Pray and work
30. The morbid Soul of Vienna

BIKIE RENTAL
IN STYLE

Once upon a time, on Bruno-Marek-Allee, stood one of the most magnificent train stations of the Austro-Hungarian Empire, Vienna's Nordbahnhof (North Station). The station is long gone, but one of the city's largest urban development projects is currently being built in its place. Car traffic plays a very minor role in this modern district concept, and so it's no wonder that since 2019 the well-known Starbike shop has found a new home here. Owner Michael Knoll has created a friendly paradise for all bike enthusiasts within some 300 square metres – it doesn't matter if you're a bike nerd or a beginner, you're welcome to advice over an espresso.

STARBIKE
BRUNO-MAREK-ALLEE 11
1020 WIEN

starbike.at

SHIMANO
SHIMANO
UNIOR
CIAO

Visitors to Vienna can benefit from a special offer: at Starbike, you can not only buy stylish bikes or have them repaired, but also rent them. Anyone who had to leave their gravel bike at home can simply borrow a sporty bike for a ride through Vienna Woods, or join one of the group city tours. Starbike is also an art gallery boasting a rare treasure: the internationally acclaimed street artist Golif has decorated a wall with one of his iconic paintings.

Zwettler
GASTHAUS zum SIEG
Zwettler
Wiener Beisl
vom Fass
Zwettler
Waldviertel pur.
Wiener Beisl
vom Fass
Zwettler
Waldviertel pur. 
KÜCHE
VON
11³⁰ – 14°°
UND VON
17°° – 21³⁰
Zwettler

A DAILY POT **OF GOULASH**

A decades-old bar, wood-panelled walls, a rustic atmosphere, and a dining room always packed with locals: The Gasthaus zum Sieg is one of the city's most beautiful and atmospheric traditional restaurants. You should really reserve a table in advance by phone, since this is the only guaranteed way to enjoy it. You'll be looking in vain for a website, Facebook, or even an Instagram page, just as you won't find a menu. There's only one dish on offer here: the best and tastiest goulash in Vienna, if not in all of Central Europe. Every day it simmers for hours in a huge pot until it reaches mouth-watering perfection. The spicy, buttery pieces of beef literally melt in your mouth. The meal is best accompanied by a freshly tapped glass of Austrian beer. No better place to dive into the culinary soul of Vienna than here!

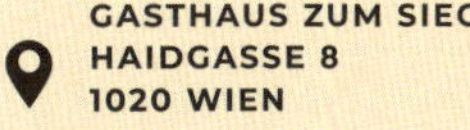

GASTHAUS ZUM SIEG
HAIDGASSE 8
1020 WIEN

+43 1 214 46 53

THREE MORE FANTASTIC TRADITIONAL VIENNESE RESTAURANTS

> Simon Schubert and Julian Lechner accurately describe their restaurant as a contemporary Viennese inn. It's hard to imagine a better way of combining local tradition with the demands of modern quality cuisine, including the occasional exotic twist. A well-deserved three Gault&Millau toques!

Reznicek
Reznicekgasse 10 – 1090 Wien
+43 1 310 44 07
*reznicek.co.at – Instagram: @_reznicek_*

> Viennese cuisine straight from the heart: Gasthaus Grünauer is a place of authentic local hospitality. Outstanding quality without trendy garnishing, a fantastic selection of Austrian wines, and one of the most comfortable dining rooms in the city.

Gasthaus Grünauer
Hermanngasse 32 – 1070 Wien
+43 1 526 40 80
gasthaus-gruenauer.at

> A skilfully renovated suburban inn. The cuisine follows in the footsteps of legendary Viennese chef Heinz Herkner. Success guaranteed: top-class Austrian cuisine is served. You can enjoy a rich selection of perfectly prepared offal dishes – there's also a highly recommended selection for vegetarians.

Pichlmaiers zum Herkner
Dornbacher Straße 123 – 1170 Wien
+43 1 480 12 28
zumherkner.at – Instagram: @pichlmaierszumherkner

ZNICEK

GASTHAUS
GRÜNAUER

PICHLMAIERS ZUM HERKNER

PHOTOS © PICHELMAIERS ZUM HERKNER

PICHLMAIERS
ZUM HERKNER

A SWIMMING POOL ON THE RIVER

Going for a swim in the heart of Vienna city centre? That's also on offer. Not directly in the Danube Canal, which winds prominently through the city, but rather on the canal, in the so-called Badeschiff (bathing ship). The name says it all – on the deck of this firmly anchored boat is a 27-metre-long pool that's unparalleled in terms of style. Here, you can relax and swim laps with a view of the venerable façade of the neo-Baroque Urania Observatory, waving to passing boats and attracting the envious glances of passers-by.

BADESCHIFF WIEN
FRANZ-JOSEFS-KAI 4/DONAUKANAL
1010 WIEN

+43 660 31 24 703

badeschiff.at

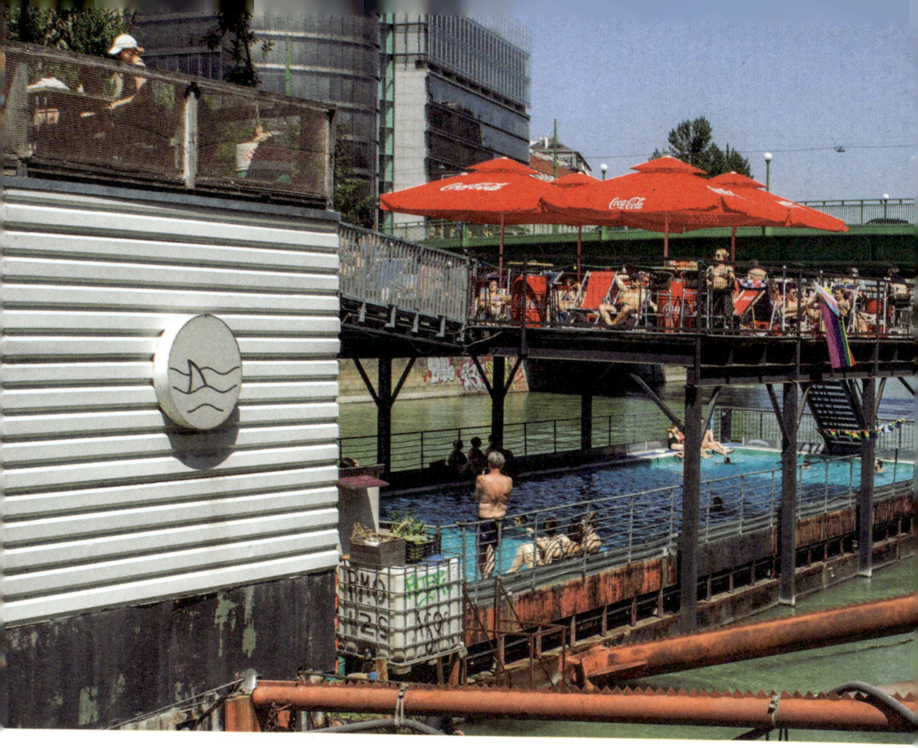
Coca-Cola
Coca-Cola

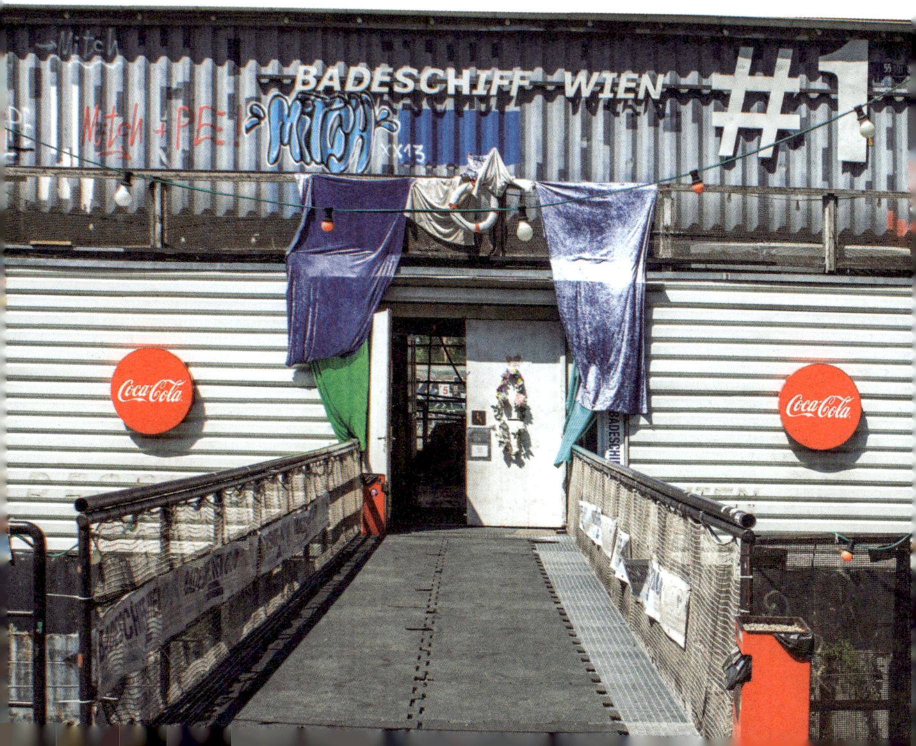
BADESCHIFF WIEN
#1
Coca-Cola
Coca-Cola

SCHÖNBRUNNER BAD

KRAPFENWALDLB

As if all that weren't extraordinary enough, the pool's offerings aren't just for summer – Austria is known for its winter sports tradition. Even if the mountains are a bit too far away from Vienna for skiing, you can enjoy curling or ice swimming on the Badeschiff, followed by a sauna session. Afterwards enjoy a glass of punch or mulled wine from the galley, and you have the perfect vacation afternoon in Vienna.

THE VERY BEST SWIMMING FUN IN VIENNA:

> Art Nouveau and architecture fans, pay attention – opposite the iconic Tichy ice cream parlour, you can swim laps in a chic Art Deco atmosphere.

Amalienbad
Reumannplatz 23 – 1100 Wien
+43 1 607 47 47 – wien.gv.at

> Swimming pool with a view – in this legendary summer pool, the whole of Vienna lies at your feet.

Krapfenwaldlbad
Krapfenwaldgasse 65-73 – 1190 Wien
+43 1 320 15 01 – wien.gv.at

> Open-air swimming pool located directly in the elegant Schönbrunn Palace gardens, where Emperor Franz Joseph learned to swim – includes a 50-metre Olympic-size pool and a fantastic restaurant.

Schönbrunner Bad
Schlosspark Schönbrunn – 1130 Wien
+43 1 817 53 53 – schoenbrunnerbad.at

AMALIENBAD

A VERY SOPHISTICATED **LUNCH**

Let's visit one of Austria's best chefs. Konstantin Filippou's extraordinarily exciting and unconventional restaurant currently boasts five Gault&Millau toques and two Michelin stars. Konstantin's cooking can be best described as the outcome of a passion for experimentation, artistic creativity, and a spectacular international career. He blends the cuisine of his Austrian and Greek ancestors in ways previously unseen. The nine-course dinner menu, sophisticated in its perfection, is an experience that will remain in the culinary memory of even the most well-travelled hardcore foodies for a very long time.

RESTAURANT KONSTANTIN FILIPPOU
DOMINIKANERBASTEI 17
1010 WIEN

+43 1 512 22 29

konstantinfilippou.com
Instagram: @konstantinfilippou

O BOUFÉS

For a somewhat less complicated yet still top-notch dining experience, you can enjoy wining and dining next door at O boufés bistro. Also, on the outskirts of Vienna, Konstantin and his friendly team at Mama Konstantina dedicate themselves to traditional Greek cuisine with their usual enthusiasm.

However, a visit to the main restaurant is recommended, especially at lunchtime: you'll rarely be able to enjoy cuisine of this level anywhere in Europe at a cheaper price than the business lunch at €69.

O BOUFÉS
DOMINIKANERBASTEI 17
1010 WIEN

+43 1 512 22 29 10
konstantinfilippou.com/oboufes
Instagram: @o.boufes

MAMA KONSTANTINA
DÖBLINGER HAUPTSTRASSE 17
1190 WIEN

+43 1 438 00 95
mamakonstantina.com
Instagram: @mamakonstantina

THE NIGHT BAR
NOT TO MISS!

Vienna has been home to truly snazzy cocktail bars ever since the American Bar, designed by architect Adolf Loos, opened in 1910. Since then, bar culture has continually reinvented itself, adopting and also rejecting trends all the time. It has kept Vienna an interesting city for night owls.

The Kleinod bar in the city centre is one of our favourite places for late-night drinks. The staff strike the right tone in conversation, and the drinks offer the perfect flavour nuances for almost every taste. The clientele is not too young, not too old, and not too homogeneous. To top it all, the decor skilfully plays with all the attributes that make for a cosy night-time retreat. Even an ancient cigarette machine is still functional and available for use.

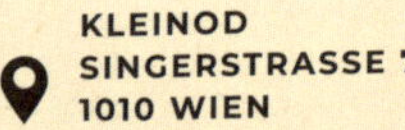

KLEINOD
SINGERSTRASSE 7
1010 WIEN

+43 664 22 36 300

kleinod-diebar.wien
Instagram: @kleinodwien

PHOTOS © NIKOLAUS MAUTNER MARKHOF

The highlights, however, are the numerous signature cocktails created by the Kleinod team – they combine detailed knowledge of the history of bar culture with a pioneering spirit of experimentation to create irresistible taste experiences. Our personal favourites are the Muffin, Apple Pie, Red Hot Chili Pepper, Thai Massage and Tyler Durden.

№ 3
№ 4

A NIGHT IN **A LUXURY DORMITORY**

Even those who don't have the budget to enjoy the grand suite (from €1,469) can still find befitting accommodation at the formidable Hotel Grand Ferdinand on Vienna's Ringstrasse. A memorable economy class experience in traditional 19th-century hospitality style is available. An antique mahogany bunkbed in a dormitory for eight people can be booked for as little as €50. The ambiance of the dormitory is reminiscent of the Orient Express or the Titanic. It really feels like a journey back in time to the golden era of glamorous travel. This elegant hotel also houses one of the best Viennese schnitzel restaurants in the city. It also has a romantic rooftop bar with a swimming pool.

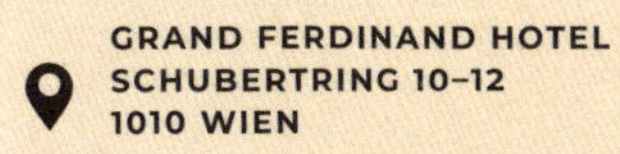

GRAND FERDINAND HOTEL
SCHUBERTRING 10-12
1010 WIEN

+43 1 91 880 0

grandferdinand.com
Instagram: @grandferdinand

TRADITIONAL CRAFTS, **SUGARY SWEET**

The art of confectionery in Vienna can look back on a centuries-old history. To this day, you can find numerous old-fashioned pastry shops and candy stores selling a wide selection of classic and reinvented delicacies. In the Zuckerlwerkstatt (sugar workshop), a beautiful tradition has been saved from extinction: the artisanal production of brightly coloured candies, available in a wide variety of colours and flavours. The sugar paste is worked using only spatulas and scissors, creating wonderfully garish and charming motifs. At the *Schaumanufaktur* (production workshop which is open to visitors) in the heart of Vienna's city centre, you can witness this truly spectacular process. Afterwards you can choose from a huge selection of sugary-sweet souvenirs.

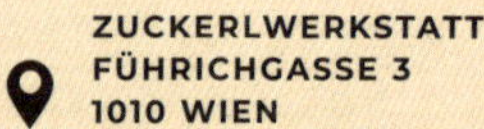

ZUCKERLWERKSTATT
FÜHRICHGASSE 3
1010 WIEN

zuckerlwerkstatt.at

© ASTRID SCHWAB

© CREA-VIA

A BOUTIQUE HOTEL **WHERE EVERY ROOM IS UNIQUE**

Spittelberg, not far from the city centre, is an atmospherically beautiful district full of historic buildings. It's a very convenient starting point for exploring the city. Why not stay here? Boutique Hotel Altstadt Vienna offers the atmosphere of a grand city residence from the time of the Habsburg monarchy, yet has unconventionally contemporary rooms curated by renowned designers from every conceivable field of art. The hotel owner's family also owns an impressive art collection, and select works from it embellish the rooms. Thus, you can enjoy your stay amidst valuable originals by Hubert Schmalix, Brigitte Kowanz, Andy Warhol, Annie Leibovitz and Friedensreich Hundertwasser, while being perfectly located for exploring the numerous art galleries in the area.

ALTSTADT VIENNA HOTEL
KIRCHENGASSE 4
1070 WIEN

+43 1 522 66 66

altstadt.at
Instagram: @altstadtvienna

HOTEL ALTSTADT VIENNA

TWO MORE CHARMING HOTELS

> Hotel Motto offers sophisticated elegance in a luxurious, impeccably renovated historical building in the middle of Vienna's main shopping street. It has a fantastic bakery, and probably the city's most beautiful rooftop restaurant.

Hotel Motto
Mariahilfer Straße 71a – 1060 Wien
+43 1 581 45 00
hotelmotto.at – Instagram: @hotelmottovienna

> Magnificent rooms covered in colourful decor, an extensive vinyl library and a world-class cocktail bar can be found at this charming boutique hotel.

Die Josefine Hotel
Esterhazygasse 33 – 1060 Wien
+43 1 588 70
hoteljosefine.at –Instagram: @diejosefinewien

DIE JOSEFINE

PHOTOS © OLIVER JISZDA

HOTEL MOTTO

ESPRESSO, SAUERKRAUT AND THE BEST CROISSANTS IN TOWN

Café Bar Espresso is one of those delightful places where time seems to have stood still. On entering you're transported back to the 1950s, when modern Italian chic slowly made its way into grey post-war Vienna. However, since Italian chic is known to be timeless, the ambiance remains as fresh in the 21st century as it did when it opened. And from 7:30 am to midnight, the restaurant offers practically everything a city dweller could need. Early in the day you can find the best croissants in town from the adjoining Ährnst organic bakery. For lunch, you'll be treated to a hearty menu, delicious tramezzini, and tasty homemade dishes made with old-style preserves from jars. Then in the evening, this place is the perfect starting point for extended expeditions into Viennese nightlife – great cocktails and trendy DJs included.

CAFÉ NATURAL WINE BAR ESPRESSO
BURGGASSE 57
1070 WIEN

+43 1 522 10 570

espresso-wien.at
Instagram: @espresso_burggasse

Schremser
Schremser
Bier

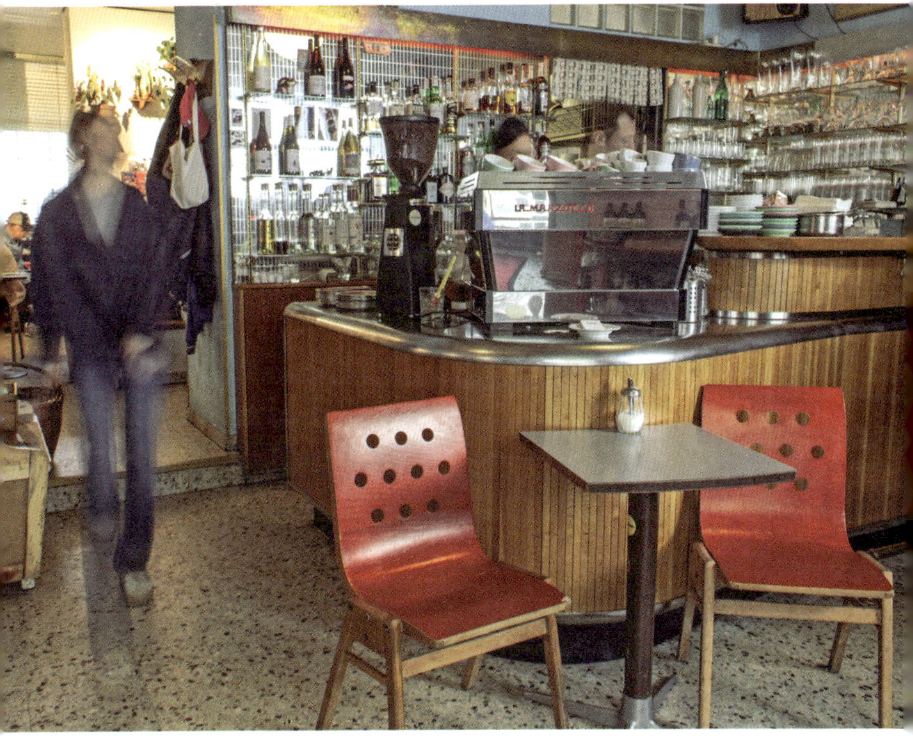

A CHAMBER OF WONDERS OF PHOTOGRAPHY

In the backyard of a former glass factory lies a place that attracts photography enthusiasts from all over the world. A magical experience for anyone interested in photography. Starting with the private collection of photographer Peter Coeln, a museum was created here in 2001. It is dedicated to the subject of photography with astonishing completeness and inspiring depth. In addition to a large number of rare and historically significant cameras, one of the last surviving examples of the earliest commercially produced camera, is on display: a daguerreotype which was produced by the Susse Frères company, and which dates back to 1839.

WESTLICHT. SCHAUPLATZ FÜR FOTOGRAFIE
WESTBAHNSTRASSE 40
1070 WIEN

from  to 

+43 1 522 66 36

westlicht.com
Instagram: @westlichtvienna

The museum collection isn't just spectacular hardware from all eras of camera technology. The approximately 120,000-piece photographic collection provides a detailed overview of the diverse eras, genres and technical formats of photography. The exhibitions, which change several times a year, introduce a balanced mix of important names and current developments in the field of photographic art, as well as a variety of interesting topics, such as the annual presentation of World Press Photos.

FRANKE & HEIDECKE BRAUNSCHWEIG
GERMANY Nr. 2423
Hans Hass
In unberühr
Tief
Die Bezwingung
der tropischen
Meere
Molden

Cameras, Lenses and Accessories
Nikon
Nippon Kogaku Japan

PURE **JOY**

Pure joy – that fittingly describes an evening visit to this outstanding restaurant. The atmosphere ranges from inviting to intimate. The extremely friendly staff convey the highest level of expertise and passion for advanced culinary arts. We recommend choosing the surprise menu (ranging from two to six courses), which suits almost everyone's budget and time available for a meal. What's served here casually bridges the gap between cleverly reimagined retro culinary traditions and sophisticated fine dining. This also applies to the fantastic cocktails, which easily eclipse the offerings of many classic bars in terms of taste.

Use of the finest regional ingredients and many home-made dishes (like the wonderful, in-house fermented miso) demonstrates how easily sustainable thinking and first-class culinary arts can go together.

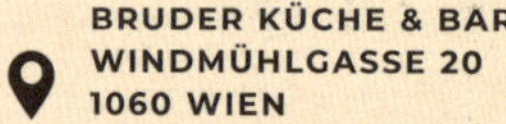

+43 664 135 13 20

bruder.xyz
Instagram: @bruder.xyz

PHOTOS © ST. CHARLES APOTHECARY

A REFUGE **FOR BODY AND SOUL**

The Saint Charles Apothecary offers a brief respite for the senses which may be overstimulated by the hustle and bustle of sightseeing. The moment you step inside, your soul breathes a sigh of relief, as a soothing scent of herbs and essential oils welcomes weary visitors.

Your attention is immediately drawn towards a spacious, dark-wood apothecary cabinet, a true original from the Habsburg era. It gives the room its old-fashioned charm. And it's not just the visual aspect where tradition meets modernity; this exceptional pharmacy combines time-honoured healing knowledge with a sustainable, holistic approach.

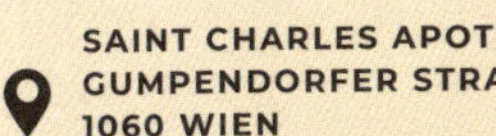
SAINT CHARLES APOTHECARY
GUMPENDORFER STRASSE 30
1060 WIEN

+43 1 586 13 63

saint-charles.eu
Instagram: @saint.charles

A product from the in-house range makes an original Vienna souvenir. We particularly recommend the house's signature perfumes, created by Viennese perfume writer and artist Paul Divjak. If you're looking for even more relaxation and wellbeing after your visit to the apothecary, simply book a beauty appointment at the Saint Charles Hideaway cosmetic studio opposite or treat yourself to a healthy snack from Saint Charles Alimentary.

ONE OF THE BEST VINTAGE FASHION SHOPS IN THE WORLD

This store features a stunning selection of luxurious vintage fashion spanning a century of haute couture. Among the spectacular pieces are an original Paco Rabanne sequin top from 1968, the swimsuit worn by Marilyn Monroe in *Gentlemen Prefer Blondes*, and a pair of lace-up boots that once belonged to Empress Sisi (who now gets a mention in this guide).

It's no wonder that Flo Vintage is considered a globally recognised institution in this business. Fashionistas such as Stella McCartney, Scarlett Johansson and Marc Jacobs are just some of its regular customers. Even the great Karl Lagerfeld has found inspiration for new creations here!

FLO VINTAGE
SCHLEIFMÜHLGASSE 15A
1040 WIEN

+43 1 586 07 73

flovintage.com
Instagram: @flovintagevienna

FELA
Bande Originale du Film
NEW-YORK
1997
PIERRE HENRY
FUTURISTIE
WHAT A WAY TO
TIGER
GOOD BOY ME
FUCKHEAD

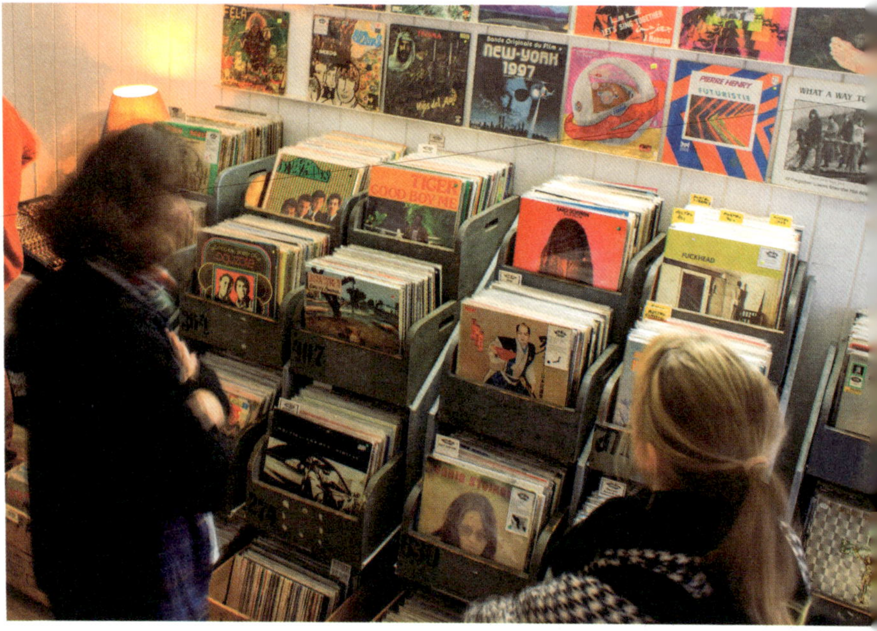

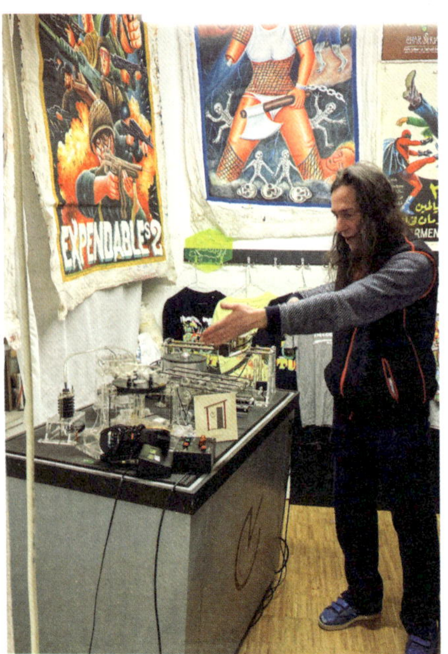

EXPENDABLES 2

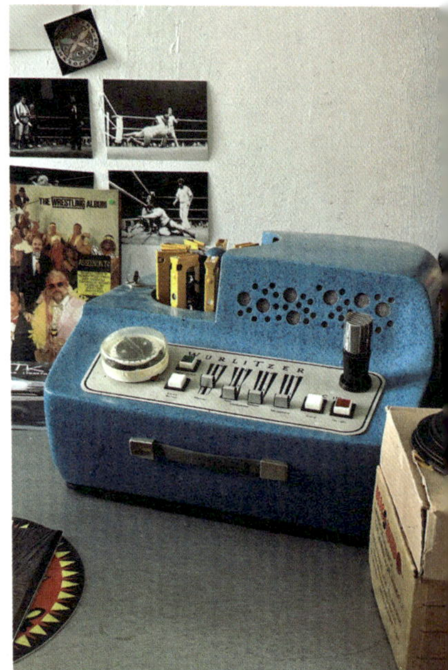

THE WRESTLING ALBUM
WURLITZER

AN AMAZING **MUSICAL TREASURE TROVE**

Albi Dornauer has spent years travelling the world in search of rare vinyl records from the 1950s-70s. He offers some of his extraordinary collection for sale in his shop, Boom Boom Records. Among many quirky things, there are records of soul girl groups from Sudan, reggae from Greenland, Soviet funk from Kazakhstan, Peruvian cumbia, psychedelic rock from Texas, and some rare collectables from the early years of hip-hop. You'll also find rare pop cultural treasures, such as hand-painted film posters from Ghana.

The shop also offers an interesting way to send holiday greetings home. The Vinylograph invented by Natascha Muhic and Christoph Freidhöfer is a cut-your-own-record machine. It lets you record live sound (or the opening bars of a future global hit?) onto 7-inch singles or musical postcards.

BOOM BOOM RECORDS & VINYLOGRAPH
SCHÖNBRUNNER STRASSE 6
1040 WIEN

Instagram: @boomboomrecordsvienna
boomboomrecordsvienna@gmail.com

vinylograph.com

Vienna is known as the city of music. That's why, we want to venture a little beyond the mainstream in this area too. We'll leave Mozart, Falco and even the Vienna Boys' Choir to the tourist masses. How about a stroll through the flea market or the numerous record stores instead? Perhaps you'll find one of these 30 rare, valuable and exceptionally cool rock, pop and jazz LPs from Vienna. The sounds of the city from the 1960s to the 1980s were just as unusual as you might expect: international yet idiosyncratic, challenging, wild, offbeat, simply irresistible!

#01 Jack's Angels – *Our Fantasy's Kingdom* [1967]
#02 The 'V'-Rangers – *Explosion* [1968]
#03 Peter Wolf – *A Change In My Life* [1969]
#04 The Masters of Unorthodox Jazz – *Overground* [1969]
#05 Misthaufen – *Dung Heap* [1971]
#06 Uzzi Förster – *Udrilitten* [1972]
#07 Joerg Siegert & Chorus Of XII – *Brain Sound: An Attempt to Record Coincidence* [1972]
#08 ORF Big Band, Johannes Fehring & The Chicks – *Same* [1972]
#09 Paternoster – *Paternoster* [1972]
#10 Lazarus – *Lazarus* [1973]
#11 Acid – *Acid* [1974]
#12 Red Devils – *Redevils* [1974]
#13 Kaplan Manfred Schwarz – *Meine Waffe ist die Gitarre* [1974]
#14 Kyrie Eleison – *The Fountain Beyond the Sunrise* [1976]
#15 Orange Power – *Orange Power* [1977]
#16 Atlas – *Atlas* [1977]
#17 Various Artists – *Wiener Blutrausch* [1979]
#18 Cultural Noise – *Aphorisms Insane* [1980]
#19 Monoton – *Monoton* [1980]
#20 Magic Mail – *Magic Mail* [1981]
#21 Various Artists – *Die Tödliche Dosis* [1981]
#22 Dämmerattacke – *Tausend Seen* [1982]
#23 Der Eiserne Vorhang – *Ohne Ausweg* [1982]
#24 Blümchen Blau – *Wie die Tiere* [1982]
#25 X-Beliebig – *X-Beliebig* [1982]
#26 Treasure Island – *Change the Prisoner* [1983]
#27 Ronnie Urini & Die letzten Poeten – *Aus den Kellern der Nacht* [1983]
#28 Bizarre Ko.Ko.Ko. – *00 Time* [1984]
#29 Timeshift – *On the Edge of Society* [1988]
#30 Astaron – *Astaron* [1988]

A TRADITIONAL VIENNESE CAFÉ WITHOUT THE TOURIST CROWDS

Long before the third coffee wave swept across Central Europe and irrevocably changed the scene, Vienna was a cosmopolitan city of coffee consumption. Traditional Viennese coffee house culture has become such an influential part of urban life that it's included on the UNESCO Intangible Cultural Heritage list.

The enchanting Café Goldegg exquisitely represents the historic beauty of Viennese coffee houses. At the same time, the establishment which was restored a few years ago, is exemplary in its tasteful, authentic renovation that avoids excessive kitsch and commercialisation. Long queues of tourists at the door are happily left to sort themselves out. The focus is instead on the true strength of the Viennese coffee house: offering customers a brief respite from their everyday lives.

CAFÉ GOLDEGG
ARGENTINIERSTR. 49
1040 WIEN

+43 1 505 91 62

cafegoldegg.at
Instagram: @cafegoldegg

CAFE
GOLDEGG

Marble tables, brass lamps, parquet floors and ebony walls bring the artistic atmosphere of Viennese Art Nouveau into the present. Billiard tables, a beautiful old stove, and an exotic and opulent back room are among the harmonious details that make this coffee house, founded in 1910, one of our absolute favourites.

THREE MORE VIENNESE CAFÉS WHERE YOU'LL ENCOUNTER MORE LOCALS THAN VISITORS

> French billiards, an outstanding selection of current newspapers and a generally very slow-paced attitude to life are offered by the wonderfully old-fashioned Café Weingartner.

Café Weingartner
Goldschlagstraße 6 – 1150 Wien
+43 1 982 43 99
weingartner.co.at – Instagram: @cafe_weingartner

> After a well-thought-out renovation, Café Schopenhauer perfectly connects the early 20th century and the present. Timeless elegance, a fantastic breakfast menu, piano playing, a bookstore in the middle of the dining room, and probably the friendliest coffee house team in all of Vienna. An absolute favourite!

Café Schopenhauer
Staudgasse 1 – 1180 Wien
+43 1 406 32 88
cafeschopenhauer.at – Instagram: @cafeschopenhauer

> This opulently furnished traditional café is located in a magnificent 19th-century city palace. The Savoy is not only a great place to relax after a visit to the Naschmarkt, but also a popular meeting place for queer Vienna with a correspondingly exciting, cosmopolitan clientele.

Café Savoy
Linke Wienzeile 36 – 1060 Wien
+43 1 430 33 04
cafe-savoy.at – Instagram: @cafesavoyvienna

CAFÉ SAVOY

CAFÉ SCHOPENHAUER

Wurzen
2,69
A-Nr. 402
Pferde-
KNOBLAUCH-Würstel
nach Alt Wiener Tradition
2,69
BIZERBA
0.006
0.332
0.00
Kakao Milch
Kakao Milch

HOPFENSCHWINGER
Keller
Pferde
Gulasch
Pferde
Gulasch
Pferde
Gulasch
HOPFENSCHWINGER
Keller

HIGH HORSE
ON A FLAT PLATE

Gumprecht is the last of Vienna's horse meat butchers – there were 600 of them once upon a time. It offers numerous horse meat products at several of the city's markets. For those hungry visitors who want a taste, we recommend the regional equivalent of the Berlin currywurst or the New York burger: the classic horse meat loaf roll. This popular Viennese fast food is always delicious at Gumprecht. It tastes especially good during a relaxed stroll through one of Vienna's beautiful markets. Our three favourite markets that offer authentic city life are: Meidlinger Markt, Viktor-Adler Markt in Favoriten district, and Floridsdorfer Markt (Schlingermarkt).

HORSEMEAT BUTCHER GUMPRECHT
pferdefleischer.at

Viktor-Adler-Markt, 1100 Wien	Meidlinger Markt, 1120 Wien	Floridsdorfer Markt, 1210 Wien
Stand 38/43	**Stand 134/135**	**Stand 60 & 69**
+43 1 606 22 29	+ 43 1 812 40 24	+43 1 270 13 22

GELATI! **GELATI!**

For some, snowdrops or hyacinths are the first signs of spring, but not for us Viennese. We declare the cold season finally over when the Tichy ice cream parlour opens its doors after the winter break in mid-March. Suddenly, people are strolling all around Reumannplatz, licking ice cream, and the proverbial Viennese grumpiness gives way to Italian lightness. Tichy is a cult in Vienna, and a visit to this wonderfully gaudy ice cream parlour with its 1950s flair is highly recommended.

Sitting in one of Vienna's most traditional ice cream parlours is an experience. Also, you can get the legendary original Viennese ice cream dumpling – among delicious classics like vanilla, strawberry and chocolate ice cream. This famous, patented creation, which has been around for decades, is worth savouring at least once in your life.

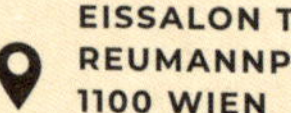

EISSALON TICHY
REUMANNPLATZ 13
1100 WIEN

+43 1 604 44 46

tichy-eissalon.at
Instagram: @eissalon_tichy

GELATO CARLO

SCHELATO

GEFRORENES

THREE OTHER TRENDY MUST-VISIT ICE CREAM SHOPS

> Carlo Maghakian used to be an advertising designer, then learned how to make outstanding ice cream from master Giacomo Schiavon in Bologna – and is now arguably one of the best *gelatieri* in Europe. Classic flavours are so pure and intense that they are in a league of their own here, and the in-house creations are simply spectacular.
Gelato Carlo
Hamerlingplatz 2 – 1080 Wien
gelatocarlo.com – Instagram: @gelato.carlo

> This charming little shop, Gefrorenes – Eis wie Damals [*Frozen – Ice Cream Like It Used To Be*], in the 18th district has been open for ten years. It offers great Italian-style ice cream, the milk ice cream is lovely and rich, but we particularly enjoy the perfectly creamy sorbets. If you'd like to know more, you can try to secure a spot at one of the coveted *gelato* workshops.
Gefrorenes - Eis wie damals
Währinger Straße 152 – 1180 Wien
+43 676 492 70 61
gefrorenes.com – Instagram: @gefrorenes_eis_wie_damals

> Schelato now has several branches and often travels to various events with a Piaggio Ape. But the original location near the Naschmarkt still exudes a friendly innovative store atmosphere. Great, handmade ice cream and always cheerful staff!
Schelato
Schleifmühlgasse 11 – 1040 Wien
schelato.at – Instagram: @schelato

#18

ORDINARY PEOPLE'S AMUSEMENT PARK

Did you know that in addition to the internationally renowned Vienna Prater, there's also a hidden vintage amusement park on the outskirts of the city? Unlike its big brother, which sits enthroned in the heart of the city and magnetically attracts thousands of tourists with its flashing lights and Ferris wheel, the Bohemian Prater is hidden in the south of Vienna on the edge of Laa Forest. Once there, visitors discover a small, anachronistic leisure paradise, far from the hustle and bustle of the big city.

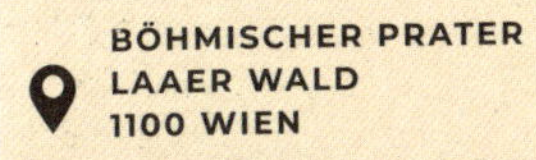

BÖHMISCHER PRATER
LAAER WALD
1100 WIEN

Instagram: @boehmischerprater

boehmischer-prater.com

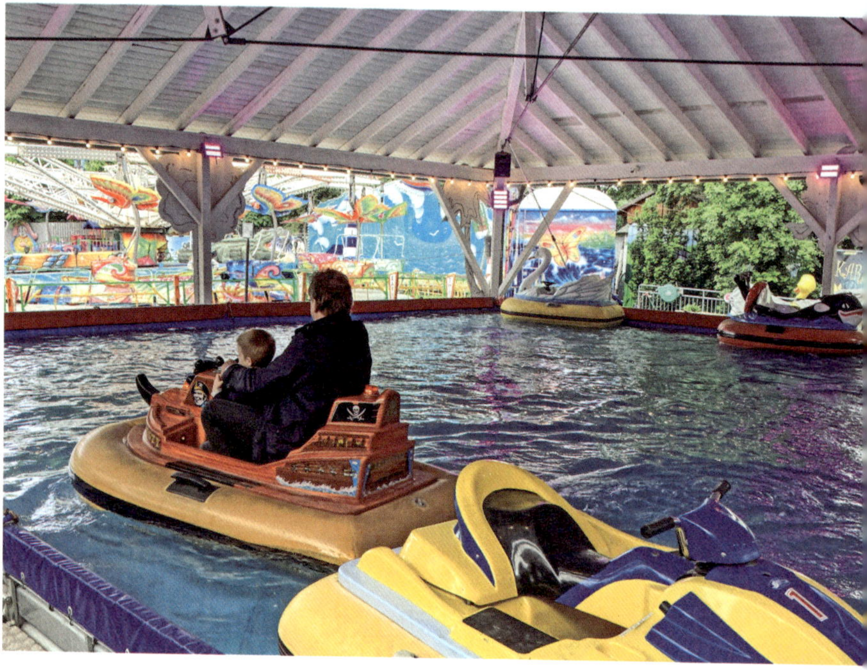

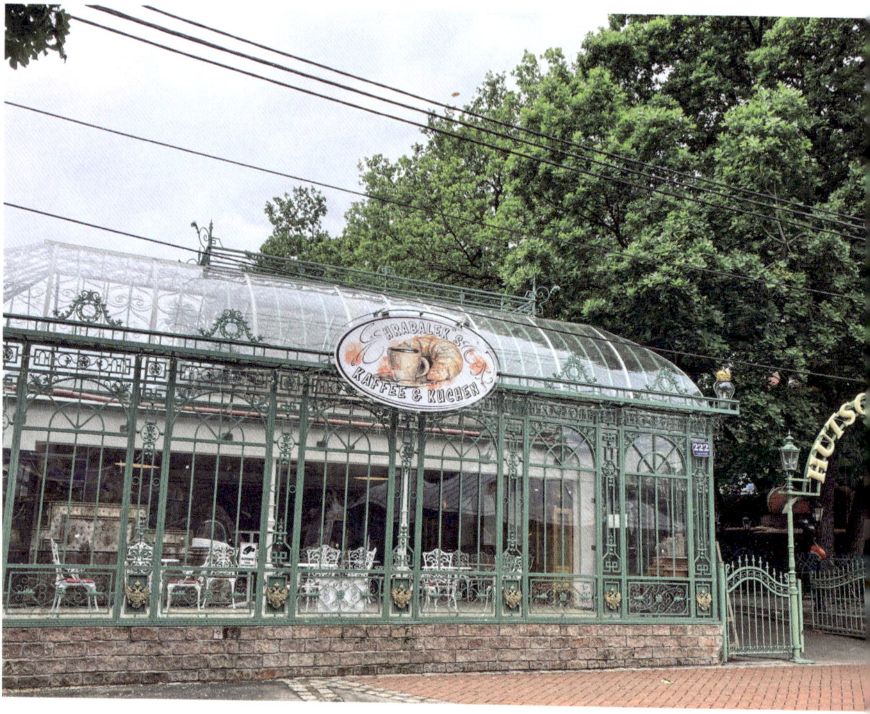
HRABALEK'S
KAFFEE & KUCHEN
222

This alternative amusement park was created over 150 years ago when exhausted Bohemian Gastarbeiter, employed in the surrounding brickworks to create the splendour of Vienna's Ringstrasse, sought a little relaxation on Sundays. They found this on daytrips to Laa Forest at inns with showman's licences, and the foundations for the Bohemian Prater were laid. Indeed, alongside quaint restaurants like the 'Werkelmann' and modern rides, you can still find a legendary carousel, said to have been personally inaugurated by Emperor Franz Joseph. The over 100-year-old 'Raupe', a bumpy roller coaster, also gives a good sense of the down-to-earth retro charm of these unconventional attractions.

A HIDDEN **RENAISSANCE GEM**

Tired of the tourist crowds at Schönbrunn Palace or Belvedere Palace, but still want to step back into the Habsburg era? Then head to the lesser known Neugebäude Palace. It's well-tucked away in Vienna's 11th district, Simmering, very close to the famous Central Cemetery.

Planned by Emperor Maximilian II as an imposing summer residence, the building remained unfinished, even to this day, after the monarch's untimely death. Nevertheless, this magnificent Renaissance palace is definitely worth a visit, and not just for its eventful history. In addition to attending special cultural events or the atmospheric Christmas market in the magnificent courtyard, a stroll in the 'Lower Garden' is always recommended.

SCHLOSS NEUGEBÄUDE
OTMAR-BRIX-GASSE 1
1110 WIEN

schlossneugebaeude.wien

The historic palace gardens are perfect for strolling in Habsburg style, and children can enjoy a giraffe swing, which is supposed to be reminiscent of the former menagerie there.

If you continue your excursion on foot for a few minutes through Simmering park, you'll reach the second gate of Vienna's Central Cemetery. From there, you can either take tram line 71 back to the city centre or – for a truly unique Habsburg end to the day – a horse-drawn carriage ride through the cemetery.

VIENNA'S 'CENTRAL PARK' ON THE SOUTHERN OUTSKIRTS

Entering the expansive Kurpark Oberlaa not only reveals one of Vienna's most impressive parks, but also a truly historic site. This place, where people now come to unwind, was a vacant lot used for brick production in the 19th century. In the 1920s, iconic silent movies such as *Sodom and Gomorrah* and *The Slave Queen* were filmed on the approximately 100-hectare site. Today, however, only names like 'Filmteichstraße' (Film Pond Street) recall those glamorous times. After the cinema era the area became a wilderness for many years. It wasn't until the 1974 International Garden Show that it was transformed into the landscaped gardens known today as Kurpark Oberlaa. Sometimes referred to as the 'Schönbrunn of the 20th century', it truly has a lot to offer.

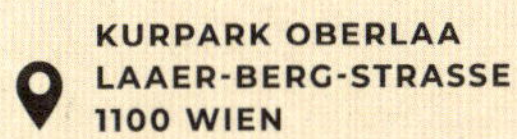

Admission free

wien.gv.at/umwelt/parks/anlagen/kurparkoberlaa

© ADOBE STOCK - ROMAN PLESKY

The perfect stroll through the park is best started at the north-east entrance. Through a small wooded area, you'll descend to the banks of the romantic 'film pond'. There, it's only natural to sit on the jetty and enjoy the view before heading to the Kurparkdiele restaurant for a portion of fries. Via the Liebesgarten (warning: Instagram potential!), you'll continue to the Japanese garden or the petting zoo. A path lined with rose bushes along Kurteich pond finally leads to the main entrance, where the Oberlaa pastry shop awaits with its cakes and other delicacies. Those who've packed their swimwear can end the day in the adjacent thermal spa and enjoy the warm sulphur thermal springs, which have been tapped since the 1960s. After an eventful few hours, the U1 line takes you back to the city in a leisurely 15-minute journey.

SLOWFOOD AT THE SNAIL FARM

Andreas Gugumuck has been breeding escargots (Roman snails) in the south of Vienna since 2008. Single-handedly he has revived a very old, long-forgotten Viennese culinary tradition. It is all done using natural methods, resource-saving techniques, and all exclusively by hand. Culinary bon vivants will find this family-run business, which has existed for more than 300 years, a wonderful example of how modern agriculture and in-depth knowledge of regional traditions can lead to first-class products.

Tours of the snail fields, a shop with delicious, canned snails, and – occasionally – truly spectacular seven-course meals prepared by award-winning chef Jürgen Winter are all on offer. The garden eatery, open every year from May onward, is particularly beautiful with its purist farm-to-table cuisine.

WIENER SCHNECKEN MANUFAKTUR GUGUMUCK
ROSIWALGASSE 44
1100 WIEN

+43 676 365 36 43

gugumuck.com
Instagram: @gugumuck

SING WITH AN AUSTRIAN FOOTBALL LEGEND

Along with a cold beer there's hearty Viennese cuisine and, occasionally, an equally down-to-earth, entertaining musical programme. A definite highlight is the annual Schlager Night with Hans Krankl – a legendary Viennese footballer who became Spain's top scorer with FC Barcelona in 1979.

ONE OF VIENNA'S **MOST BEAUTIFUL BEER GARDENS**

Halfway between the city centre and the outskirts, you'll find one of Vienna's most beautiful beer gardens. Schutzhaus Zukunft is located in the middle of an allotment garden development established in 1920, and where a piece of the city's interwar history has been preserved. And this allotment garden settlement is, in turn, located in the district with the highest proportion of immigrants, people who have shaped Vienna for centuries and helped turn it into the vibrant cultural melting pot it is today. Thus, anyone who wants to experience what the city is like, away from clichés and overtourism, will find a perfect spot on one of the wooden benches surrounded by ancient trees.

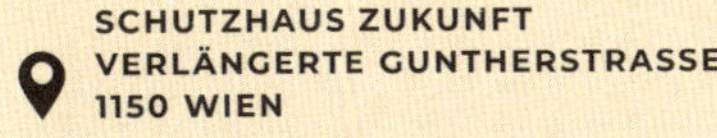

SCHUTZHAUS ZUKUNFT
VERLÄNGERTE GUNTHERSTRASSE
1150 WIEN

+43 1 982 01 27

schutzhaus-zukunft.at

LET IT **SNOW!**

At the end of the 19th century, surgical instrument mechanic Erwin Perzy I wanted to develop a new, particularly bright operating light – instead he invented one of the most popular and copied travel souvenirs of all time: the 'glass globe with snow effect'. To this day, the small family business produces 300,000 snow globes per year, half of which are exported to Japan. The range of motifs offered is vast, and some of them are extraordinarily quirky and humorous. With the exception of the glass globes, all the individual parts are manufactured at the in-house workshop and assembled by hand on-site. Custom-made items can also be ordered.

The charming shop also serves as a museum. It displays historical production equipment and rare special editions – such as a snow globe made for US President Barack Obama's visit to Vienna.

ORIGINAL WIENER SCHNEEKUGELMANUFAKTUR
SCHUMANNGASSE 87
1170 WIEN

+43 1 486 43 41 | schneekugel.at

die ganze Welt

BIG
IN JAPAN

Vienna is full of surprises. Who'd have guessed, for example, that a little piece of Tokyo was hidden in the middle of the upmarket Döbling district? A Japanese park designed by landscape architect Ken Nakajima in the 1990s stretches across an area of almost 5,000 square metres. Created as a symbol of friendship between Vienna and the Tokyo district of Setagaya, this is a place where you can stroll and linger in an authentic Japanese atmosphere, not just during cherry blossom season. The inscription on the stone next to the main entrance points the way: Furomon, the Japanese word for 'paradise', is carved there. And truly, it is almost like a Haruki Murakami novel where you leave your everyday life behind in an instant and find yourself in another world. Curved paths, artfully trimmed trees from both cultures, a teahouse, a pond with koi, the steady trickle of a waterfall – all this makes not only Japanophiles' hearts beat faster.

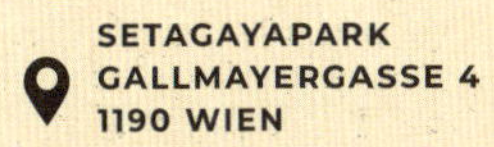

SETAGAYAPARK
GALLMAYERGASSE 4
1190 WIEN

Admission free

wien.gv.at/umwelt/parks/anlagen/setagayapark

© ADOBE STOCK / THE OBLIQUE VIEW

THE OLDEST RESTAURANT IN THE CITY

The history of this beautiful inn begins in the 12th century. Parts of the exceedingly well-maintained historic building date back to the Middle Ages. They were later converted into a magnificent Baroque palace. In this picturesque setting, traditional Viennese and imperial-royal cuisine is served, using regional ingredients of exceptional quality.

In summer, the outdoor dining area is the perfect suburban oasis for enjoying a delicious dinner in a relaxed and cosy atmosphere. To get in the mood, we recommend a refreshing glass of white wine beforehand at the adjacent Mayer Winery, whose wines are among the finest in Austria.

PFARRWIRT RESTAURANT
PFARRPLATZ 5
1190 WIEN

+43 1 370 73 73

pfarrwirt.com
Instagram: @mayerampfarrplatz.

PRIVAT
GRUNDSTÜCK

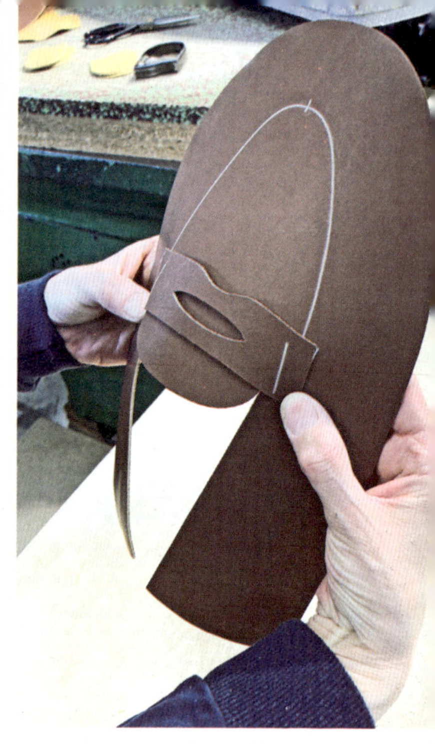

LUXURY FOOTWEAR IN A 16TH-CENTURY CASTLE

Premium shoe manufacturer Ludwig Reiter makes first-class products in a charming 16th-century castle. Nearly 100 pairs of classic Goodyear welted men's and women's shoes are handcrafted daily in the former stables. Provided there are at least five people and a suitable time, Joseph Potyka-Zeiler, a great-great-grandson of the company founder, will explain in a knowledgeable and entertaining manner how this footwear of the highest quality is made.

A visit to the factory outlet, where you can inspect and try on the fine pieces in a suitable setting, is definitely worthwhile. With a bit of luck, you might even find a rare one-off or some attractively priced leftover stock.

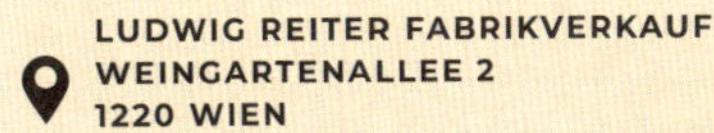

+43 1 255 93 00-61	ludwig-reiter.com Booking the guided tour: fuehrung@ludwig-reiter.com	Instagram: @ludwig_reiter

THE HEART OF CENTRAL EUROPE AT YOUR FEET

If you find yourself with some time to escape the hustle and bustle of the city centre, we recommend a bus or taxi ride to Gallitzinberg, located in the suburbs. After climbing the 183 steps of the Jubilee Tower (Jubiläumswarte), you'll be rewarded with a breathtaking panoramic view of the metropolis, as well as the famous Vienna Woods stretching westward. On particularly clear days, you can even glimpse the distant snow-capped peaks of the Alps, whose north-easternmost tops mark the boundary of the Vienna Woods.

This charming observation tower was opened in 1956. The perfect starting point for a few relaxing hours in this vast recreational area – it will give you first-hand experience of one of Vienna's qualities most cherished by locals and visitors alike: it's only a few steps from one of Europe's largest and most vibrant cities to one of the continent's most magnificent nature reserves.

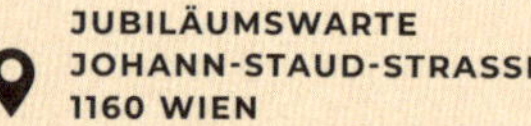

A CHURCH THAT MAY HAVE **INSPIRED MINECRAFT**

Vienna is a city full of spectacular churches. Almost every visitor has heard of the 900-year-old St Rupert's Church, the world-famous St Stephen's Cathedral, and 'the Votivkirche', which has been beautifully renovated in recent years. But there are several hidden gems among the city's approximately 300 churches. One of the most astonishing is located on the western outskirts of the city: Oberbaumgarten Parish Church. This Catholic church and pastoral care centre dedicated to the Four Evangelists is a fascinating masterpiece of post-war sacred architecture.

The main element of this reinforced concrete building is the square or cube. The consistent implementation of this concept throughout the entire church complex creates a building of captivating logic and overwhelming structure. This geometrical shape is implemented througout the interior, down to the smallest detail. This, combined with an ingenious lighting design, leads to a remarkably dense atmosphere. It will likely touch the hearts of agnostic architecture enthusiasts as much as those of devout Christians.

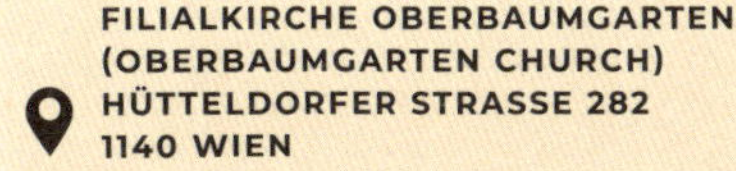

FILIALKIRCHE OBERBAUMGARTEN
(OBERBAUMGARTEN CHURCH)
HÜTTELDORFER STRASSE 282
1140 WIEN

Admission free

+43 676 578 82 98

PRAY
AND WORK

Just south of Vienna is the 135-year-old St Gabriel Mission House. Only a few members of the order still live and work in the monastery today; at its peak, there were over 650 missionaries living there. The majority of the vast mission grounds stood empty for many years until new uses were considered a few years ago. Today, St Gabriel's is once again full of life. The Hotel Gabrium is a classy hidden gem and a relaxing base for exciting days in Vienna. An organic farmer tends the monastery gardens and offers first-class agricultural products directly from the farm. Right next door, a fantastically well-stocked delicatessen, a cooking school, and a coffee roastery with its own coffee shop provide further culinary delights.

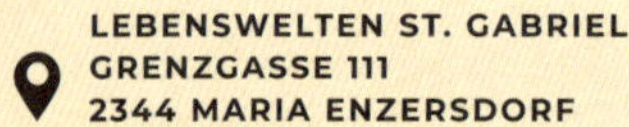

LEBENSWELTEN ST. GABRIEL
GRENZGASSE 111
2344 MARIA ENZERSDORF

+43 660 549 83 45 | lebenswelten-stgabriel.at

PHOTOS © HOTEL GABRIUM

© HOTEL CABRIUM

The rest of the facilities aren't exactly what you'd expect to find in a monastery: a CrossFit gym, a huge bookstore, a bicycle repair shop, shiatsu, and physiotherapy, as well as photography, painting, and ceramics studios. For those who need to attend to some work while travelling, there's even a co-working space.

The most beautiful part of the complex is in the middle of the old gardens surrounding the monastery: the incredibly romantic and atmospheric cemetery.

Br. Markus Koch
1905
R.I.P.
P. Lambert Koch

THREE PARTICULARLY BEAUTIFUL CULINARY EXPERIENCES IN ST. GABRIEL:

> The former sommelier Rudi Skala offers a delightful culinary selection: cheese from Austria's finest restaurant, 230 exceptional rare wines, and exquisite delicacies from small producers across Europe.

Skala Wein & Kost im Alten Bauernhof
Grenzgasse 111/7/7/10 – 2340 Maria Enzersdorf
+43 660 709 66 33
weinundkost.at
Instagram: @skala_wein_kost

> At Robert Dannbauer's cooking studio, you can learn and refine a variety of kitchen skills: baking bread and pizza, making your own cheese, or cooking an authentic Japanese ramen soup.

Kochatelier St. Gabriel
Grenzgasse 111/9/8 – 2340 Maria Enzersdorf
+43 676 359 09 10
kochatelier.at
Instagram: @kochateliersanktgabriel

> At Deluke, premium specialty coffees from the world's best growing regions have been roasted since 2015. More than twenty varieties are available, and the stylish coffee bar offers the chance to try the current 'Coffee of the Week.'

Deluke Coffee
Grenzgasse 111/11/3 – 2340 Maria Enzersdorf
office@deluke.coffee
deluke.coffee
Instagram: @delukecoffee

SKALA WEIN & KOST
M ALTEN BAUERNHOF

KOCHATELIER
ST. GABRIEL

DELUKE COFFEE

Unbekannt

THE MORBID SOUL OF VIENNA

A persistent cliché about Vienna is that it's world capital of the morbid: we Viennese are often said to have a particularly close relationship with death. Anyone who has ever visited the Cemetery of the Nameless (Friedhof der Namenlosen) will understand the fascination with this place. Even Hollywood has fallen under its spell. In his cult film about Vienna, *Before Sunrise*, American director Richard Linklater not only sent his heroes Jesse and Céline through the picturesque city centre, but also to this cemetery on the outskirts. This is the final resting place for all the (mostly) unidentified dead who washed up as waterborne corpses from the then unregulated Danube between 1840 and 1940. The simple iron crosses, often bearing the inscription *Nameless or Unknown*, memorialise the fate of the deceased, and make this disused cemetery one of Vienna's most beautiful spiritual sites.

FRIEDHOF DER NAMENLOSEN
(CEMETERY OF THE NAMELESS)
ALBERNER HAFENZUFAHRTSTRASSE
1110 WIEN

Admission free

+43 660 6003023
friedhof-der-namenlosen.at

We never reveal the 31st address
in the 'Soul of' series because it's strictly confidentia
Up to you to find it!

IN THE CELLARS OF THE NIGHT

On weekends, you might find yourself waiting in line outside an inconspicuous entrance on the corner of Berggasse and Wasagasse to immerse yourself in one of the city's most beautiful and wildest party cellars. All you need to gain entry is a bit of luck and allure ...

During the week, when things are less busy, a charming, well-run bar awaits. Be warned, it fills up quickly as the hours go by and night arrives. For us, this is one of the greatest spots in Vienna nightlife, a relaxed underground resort where the promise of sinful nocturnal excesses always wafts through the dimly lit rooms.

This book was created by:
Wolfgang Reitter and Barbara Kadletz, authors
Georg Moehrke, photographer
Ivett Galambos, illustrator
Emmanuelle Willard Toulemonde, layout
Sonny Alexander, translation
Sigrid Newman, editing
Kimberly Bess, proofreading
Mado de La Quintinie, publishing

You can write to us at info@editionsjonglez.com
Follow us on Instagram: @editionsjonglez

THANKS

From the same publisher

Photo Books

Abandoned America: The Age of Consequences
Abandoned Asylums
Abandoned Australia
Abandoned Belgium
Abandoned Churches: Unclaimed Places of Workship
Abandoned Cinemas of the World
Abandoned France
Abandoned Germany
Abandoned Lebanon
Abandoned Italy
Abandoned Japan
Abandoned Spain
Abandoned USSR
Abandoned World - An AI-generated exploration
After the Final Curtain: The Fall of the American Movie Theater
After the Final Curtain: America's Abandoned Theaters
Baikonur - Vestiges of the Soviet Space Program
Cinemas - A French Heritage
Chernobyl's Atomic Legacy - 25 years after disaster
Clickbait - A visual journey through AI-generated stories
Destination: Wellness - Our 35 best places in the world to make a pause
Forbidden Places - Exploring our Abandoned Heritage
Forbidden France
Forgotten Heritage
Parisian Theatres
Oblivion
Secret Sacred Sites
Unusual Hotels Europe
Unusual Hotels - World
Unusual Hotels UK & Ireland
Unusual Nights in Paris
Unusual Shopping in Paris
Unusual Wines
Venice deserted
Venise from the skies

'Soul of' Guides

Soul of Amsterdam - A guide to the 30 best experiences
Soul of Athens - A guide to 30 exceptional experiences
Soul of Barcelona - 30 experiences
Soul of Berlin - A guide to the 30 best experiences
Soul of Brussels - A guide to exceptional experiences
Soul of Detroit - A guide to exceptional experiences
Soul of Kyoto - A guide to exceptional experiences
Soul of Lisbon - A guide to exceptional experiences
Soul of Los Angeles - A guide to 30 exceptional experiences
Soul of Marrakesh - A guide to 30 exceptional experiences
Soul of Marseille - A guide to exceptional experiences
Soul of Milan - A guide to exceptional experiences
Soul of New York - A guide to 30 exceptional experiences
Soul of Paris - 30 experiences
Soul of Rome - A guide to exceptional experiences
Soul of Tokyo - A guide to exceptional experiences
Soul of Venice - A guide to 30 exceptional experiences

Atlas

Atlas of forbidden places
Atlas of geographical curiosities
Atlas of extreme weather
Atlas of unusual wines

Secret Atlas

London – The Secret Atlas
New York – The Secret Atlas
Paris – The Secret Atlas
Venice – The Secret Atlas

'Secret' Guides

Secret Amsterdam
Secret Bali - An unusual guide
Secret Bangkok
Secret Barcelona
Secret Bath - An unusual guide
Secret Belfast
Secret Berlin
Secret Boston - An unusual guide
Secret Brighton - An unusual guide
Secret Brooklyn
Secret Brussels
Secret Budapest
Secret Buenos Aires
Secret Campania
Secret Cape Town
Secret Copenhagen
Secret Corsica
Secret Dolomites
Secret Dublin - An unusual guide
Secret Edinburgh - An unusual guide
Secret Florence
Secret French Riviera
Secret Geneva
Secret Glasgow
Secret Granada
Secret Helsinki
Secret Istanbul
Secret Johannesburg
Secret Kuala Lumpur
Secret Lisbon
Secret Liverpool - An unusual guide
Secret London - An unusual guide
Secret London - Unusual Bars & Restaurants
Secret Los Angeles - An unusual guide
Secret Louisiana
Secret Madrid
Secret Mexico City
Secret Milan
Secret Montreal - An unusual guide
Secret Naples
Secret New Orleans - An unusual guide
Secret New York - An unusual guide
Secret New York - Curious Activities
Secret New York - Hidden Bars & Restaurants
Secret Normandy
Secret Paris
Secret Potsdam
Secret Prague
Secret Provence
Secret Rio de Janeiro
Secret Rome
Secret Seville
Secret Singapore
Secret Stockholm
Secret Sussex - An unusual guide
Secret Tokyo
Secret Tuscany
Secret Venice
Secret Vienna
Secret Washington DC - An unusual guide
Secret York - An unusual guide

Follow us on Facebook and Instagram

Registration of copyright: October 2025 – Edition: 01
ISBN: 978-2-36195-811-4
Printed in Bulgaria by Dedrax